T0197531

No More Cancer For Me!

Written and Illustrated by

Jennifer K. Okubo

AuthorHouse™
1663 Liberty Drive
Bloomington, IN 47403
www.authorhouse.com
Phone: 1 (833) 262-8899

Because of the dynamic nature of the Internet, any web addresses or links contained in this book may have changed
since publication and may no longer be valid. The views expressed in this work are solely those of the author and do not
necessarily reflect the views of the publisher, and the publisher hereby disclaims any responsibility for them.

Any people depicted in stock imagery provided by Getty Images are models,
and such images are being used for illustrative purposes only.
Certain stock imagery © Getty Images.

This book is printed on acid-free paper.

ISBN: 978-1-4490-0408-8 (sc)

Print information available on the last page.

Published by AuthorHouse 10/21/2020

authorHOUSE®

I DEDICATE THIS BOOK TO MY FAVORITE SUPER HEROES!

CONNOR, THE STRONGEST KID I KNOW!

TRACY, THE WOMAN WHO HAD ROLLERCOASTER RIDES OF LIFE AND HELD ON TIGHT WITH A SMILE ON HER FACE. I AM PROUD AND HONORED TO BE HER SISTER! RIDE ON, GIRL!

BRIAN, HE RODE THAT ROLLERCOASTER OF LIFE WHILE SERVING OUR COUNTRY EVERYDAY! GREAT AND KIND MAN!

I CAN'T FORGET COLIN AND CAMERON, THE SUPER KIDS!

MY HUSBAND, WHO STANDS BY MY SIDE THROUGH ALL MY ADVENTURES!

MY SON, KYLE, HE IS SERVING IN THE US MARINES. HE MAKES ME VERY PROUD!

I AM SO HAPPY THAT THEY ARE A PART OF MY LIFE AND A PART OF THIS WORLD. THEY MAKE IT A BETTER PLACE TO LIVE!

YOU CAN ACCOMPLISH ANYTHING IN LIFE AS LONG AS YOU TRY!

MY NAME IS CONNOR. WHEN I WAS THREE YEARS OLD, I WOKE UP AND WASN'T FEELING VERY WELL. I TOLD MY MOM THAT I COULDN'T STAND ON MY LEGS. MY MOM CALLED THE DOCTOR RIGHT AWAY.

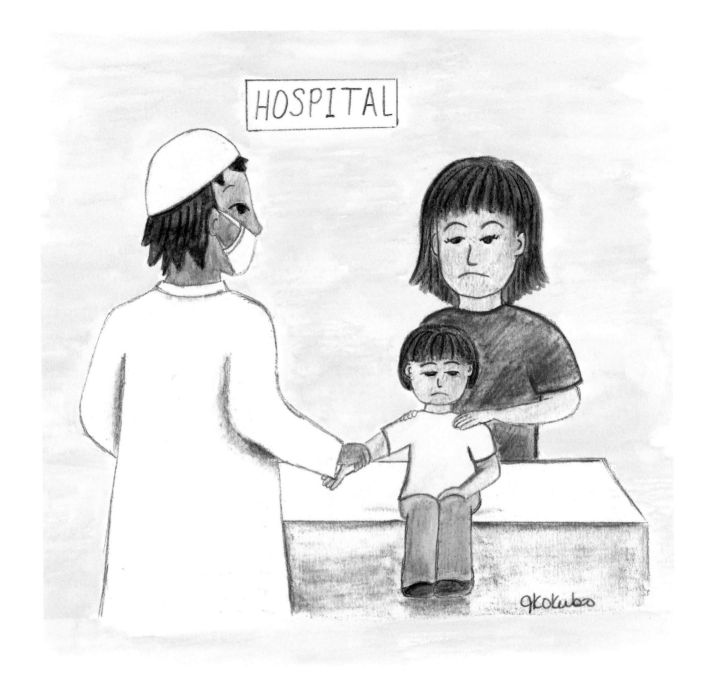

WE WENT TO THE HOSPITAL AND THEY TOOK MY BLOOD FOR TESTS.

THE TEST RESULTS WERE THAT I HAD SOME KIND OF CANCER CALLED LEUKEMIA. WE WERE ALL VERY SAD.

THE DOCTORS AND NURSES TOLD ME THAT I CAN GET THE CANCER OUT OF MY BODY. I HAD TO DO EVERYTHING THEY TOLD ME TO DO.

I FOUND OUT THAT I WAS NOT THE ONLY ONE WHO HAD CANCER. I MET A LOT OF CHILDREN WHO HAD THE SAME DISEASE. IT HELPED THAT I WAS NOT ALONE.

THE DOCTOR GAVE ME A MEDICINE CALLED CHEMO. MY BODY GOT PUFFY AND MY HAIR FELL OUT. I FOUND OUT THAT I HAVE A BEAUTIFUL ROUND HEAD, JUST LIKE MY DAD.

I HAD TO STAY IN THE HOSPITAL A LOT. ALL THE DOCTORS AND NURSES WERE VERY KIND TO ME.

THE OTHER KIDS WHO WERE SICK WITH CANCER WERE ALSO VERY NICE TO ME. SOME KIDS TOLD ME WHAT TO EXPECT, WHICH HELPED A LOT.

ALL THE CANCER KIDS AND THEIR FAMILIES BECOME ONE BIG HAPPY
FAMILY. WE WERE ALL HERE TO BATTLE CANCER TOGETHER! EVERYONE
HELPS EACH OTHER!

MY BROTHERS, COLIN AND CAMERON, ARE GREAT. WHEN THEY GOT BIGGER WE PLAYED ALL THE TIME. IF I WAS IN THE HOSPITAL, THEY WOULD COME AND VISIT ME. WE WOULD ALWAYS GO INTO THE PLAYROOM AND IT MADE ME SMILE.

ONE TIME WHEN I WAS IN THE HOSPITAL MY AUNTY JENN WENT TO MY HOUSE. SHE PAINTED MY FAVORITE SUPER HEROES ON MY BEDROOM WALL. IT WAS SO COOL!

SOME DAYS THE CANCER REALLY MADE ME SICK AND SAD. OTHER DAYS
I WAS HAPPY AND FEELING FINE.

WHEN I WAS FEELING BETTER I WENT ON TRIPS. I MADE A WISH TO
GO TO A BIG AMUSEMENT PARK. MY DREAM CAME TRUE AND WE HAD
SO MUCH FUN!

SOMETIMES I WENT TO SPECIAL CAMPS WITH OTHER CANCER KIDS.
THE SIBLINGS OF THE CHILDREN WITH CANCER EVEN GET THEIR OWN
SPECIAL WEEK. MY BROTHERS LOVE TO GO! WE ALWAYS HAVE SO MUCH
FUN BECAUSE THEY HAVE SO MANY ACTIVITIES TO DO. MY FAVORITE
THING TO DO AT CAMP IS FISH.

IT REALLY MADE ME SAD WHEN MY DAD HAD TO LEAVE FOR A WHILE. HE WENT TO FLY HIS HELICOPTER IN THE WAR. HE IS A MAJOR IN THE NATIONAL GUARD. I AM GLAD HE CAME BACK SAFE.

THEN MY MOM WENT BACK TO SCHOOL AND BECAME A NURSE TO HELP THE CANCER KIDS. JUST LIKE ALL THE DOCTORS AND NURSES HELPED ME.

IT TOOK A LONG TIME TO GET THE CANCER OUT OF ME. BUT WE DID IT! I HAVE BEEN IN REMISSION FOR FIVE YEARS NOW!

MY MOM AND DAD LET ME GROW MY HAIR LONG AND I LOVE TO PLAY
BASEBALL. I STILL GET TO GO TO THE SPECIAL CANCER CAMPS AND SEE
ALL MY FRIENDS.

MY WHOLE FAMILY MADE LOTS OF FRIENDS WITH CANCER IN THEIR LIVES. WE HAVE PARTIES ALL THE TIME SO WE CAN SEE THEM. WE WILL LOVE THEM FOREVER.

NO MORE CANCER FOR ME! I BEAT IT AND SO CAN YOU!

Printed in the United States
By Bookmasters